Copyright © 2013 by B

Disclaimer/Legal Stuff: The author their best efforts in preparing this publication. The author and publisher make no representation or warranties with respect to the accuracy, applicability, fitness, or completeness of the contents of this publication.

The material contained in this publication is provided for information purposes only!

Therefore, if you wish to apply ideas contained in this publication, you are taking full responsibility for your actions. The views expressed are those of the author alone, and should not be taken as expert instruction or commands. The reader is responsible for his or her own actions. Neither the author nor the publisher assume any blame or liability whatsoever on the behalf of the purchaser or reader of these materials. Any perceived slight of any individual or organization is purely unintentional. The author and publisher disclaim any warranties (express or implied), merchantability, or fitness for any particular purpose. The author and publisher shall in no event be held liable to any party for any direct, indirect, punitive, special, incidental or other consequential damages arising directly or indirectly from any use of this material, which is provided "as is", and without warranties.

No part of this book may be reproduced in any form without permission in writing from the author. This book contains material protected under International and Federal Copyright laws and Treaties. Any unauthorized reprint or use of this material is prohibited. Unauthorized duplication or distribution of this material in any form is strictly prohibited. No part of this publication may be reproduced, stored in a retrieval system or transmitted in any form or by any means, electronic, mechanical, photocopying, recording or otherwise, without prior written permission from the author/publisher.

INTRODUCTION

"Believe with all of your heart that you will do what you were made to do."
Orison Swett Marden

Thank you kindly for purchasing this recipe book (the 1st in a Series) and I thank you from the bottom of my heart for helping me to make in a difference in other's lives. Your thoughtful and positive reviews are greatly appreciated.

My main focus for this book is what I hope to accomplish with it (and the others following this). Making a difference is something I am driven to do and this is a way I know I can accomplish that, my sincere thanks to all of you who will help me accomplish my dream.

20% of the proceeds are going to be donated to two difference causes...10% to each of the following:

The *first* being the Cancer Society as that is what ended up taking Joan's life. It is what also took my dad's life this past November 25th, 2012.

The *second* is Food Banks. There are too many people needing a meal and while most of us take it for granted, I feel the need to help those in need and those who dedicate their lives to helping others. Every small act helps.

The recipes were given to me from my mother-in-law, Joan before she passed away nearly twenty years ago. Joan was from Sheffield and came over to Canada as a war bride. Staying close to tradition meant a lot to her and she would be happy knowing that others will be able to enjoy her recipes. She made the best Christmas cake in the world. If you follow that recipe you will be able to see for yourself how amazing it is....dark, moist with flavour bursting at every little bite. It truly gives a new meaning to fruit cake. Yum!

While the recipes may not be new and spectacular to some of you, they are simple and delicious and do conform to the conventional English cooking. As all you veteran cooks know, you add the ingredients, a dash here, and a pinch there; the recipe stored upstairs in your mind. That was the same with Joan, so please forgive me if some of the recipes leave something for your imagination. I have tried to make them as complete as possible. Over the years we've experimented with them and I encourage you to do the same. Personally, we love a lot of heat and zest to our foods and found that adding a little "spice" to anything can make it your own and will certainly give each recipe your own special touch.

DEDICATION

This book is first dedicated to God. Thank you for all your blessings & favours.

To Joan, for giving us these great recipes...you are still sadly missed.

To my dad who passed away in November. Dad I love & miss you terribly. There isn't a moment that goes by where I wish that I could talk to you, hear your voice and give you a hug. Thank you for giving me your artistic talent, your encouragement and support for everything I did.

Last but not least, this is also dedicated to my husband Michael and my fur babies (Keysha, Blue, Tess, Shamrock & Gabrielle). Thank you for your love, strength and support, I truly couldn't have made it without you. Love you always!

Table of Contents

DEDICATION 4

CHRISTMAS CAKE 7

ALMOND PASTE 8

ROYAL ICING 9

CHUTNEY 11

OLD FASHIONED CHUTNEY 12

WEDDING CAKE 13

SHEPHERD'S PIE 15

BREAD PUDDING 17

CHRISTMAS PUDDING 18

SCONES 20

SHORTBREAD 21

TRIFLE 22

IRISH STEW 24

WELSH RAREBIT 25

APPLE CIDER 26

FISH AND CHIPS 27

COOKING CONVERSION CHARTS 29

Christmas Cake

Ingredients:

- 2 cups Flour
- Pinch of Salt
- 1 tsp. Baking Powder
- 1.5 cups (12 oz.) Lard/Butter or Shortening
- .5 cups Sugar
- 0.5 cup Almonds *(ground or chopped)*
- 1 cup Sultanas
- 1 cup Raisins
- 1.5 cups Currants
- 0.5 cup Glace Cherries
- 0.5 cup Candied Peel
- Zest of 1 Lemon
- Grated 0.5 Nutmeg
- 4 Eggs
- 0.5 cup Milk
- 1 wineglassful Brandy

Method:

- Preheat the oven to 350°F (176°C).

- Wash the sultanas, currants and raisins.
- Cut the cherries in half and shred the candied peel.
- Mix the flour, salt, and baking powder in a big bowl.
- Cut the cold butter/lard into ¼ inch pieces.
- Add all the dry ingredients and the butter/lard 'chips' to the flour mixture and mix it well.
- Whisk the eggs in another bowl. Gradually add brandy to the eggs.
- Stir the milk into the egg mixture.
- Add the egg mixture to the flour/cake mixture. This moistens the cake mixture.
- Pour the mixture into a well-greased and lined cake tin.
- Bake for the first 20 minutes at 350°F (176°C).
- Bake at 300°F (150°C) for the next 4 – 4.5 hrs.
- Garnish and serve the cake with a layer of Almond Paste (about 1 inch thick) and then coat it with a layer of Royal Icing (*recipes follow*).

ALMOND PASTE

Ingredients:

- 2 cups Almonds *(ground)*
- 2 cups Castor Sugar
- 2 Eggs
- Few drops of Almond Essence

- 1 tbsp. of flavoring (orange flower water or rose water)

Method:

- Mix the almonds and sugar.
- Add the flavoring and essence (for taste and color, as preferred).
- Whisk the eggs and add to the mixture. Knead it well.
- Place the paste on the cake and roll level with rolling pin.

ROYAL ICING

Ingredients:

- 1 cup Icing Sugar
- 2 Egg Whites
- Lemon Juice *(as required)*

Method:

- Sift the sugar.
- Whisk the egg whites.
- Add some of the lemon juice and the sugar to the egg whites.
- Whisk the icing mixture until it becomes smooth and white. If it becomes too stiff, add more lemon juice.
- Keep the icing covered with a wet cloth until it is used.

Tips:

- The taste of the cake improves over time. Best to make it one or two months before it is needed.

- The butter/lard should be cold before cutting. Take it out of the fridge 30 min before it is required. This helps to fluff the pastry/dough during cooking.

CHUTNEY

Ingredients:

- 8 cups (1.8 kg) Apples *(peeled and cored)*
- 4 cups Sultanas *(finely chopped)*
- 0.5 cups (8 tbsp.) Garlic *(finely chopped)*
- 0.5 tbsp. Cayenne/Red Pepper or Chili Flakes/Powder
- 4 cups Brown Sugar
- 0.5 cups Green Ginger/0.25 cups Ginger *(ground)*
- 4 cups (1 liter) Vinegar
- Salt *(to taste)*

Method:

- In a saucepan, boil the brown sugar and cored apples to the consistency of jam.
- In a bowl, mix all the other ingredients except the vinegar.
- Add the bowl's contents to the saucepan and boil for another 10 minutes.
- Pour the mixture into a jar while it is still hot.
- Mix it well with vinegar while adding salt to taste.
- Bottle the chutney when cold.

Old Fashioned Chutney

Ingredients:

- 30 cups Apples *(peeled and cored)*
- 3 cups Brown Sugar
- 0.5 cup Spanish/Red Onions *(finely chopped)*
- 0.5 cup Garlic *(finely chopped)*
- 0.5 cup Mustard Seeds
- 0.5 cup Salt
- 1 cup Raisins *(stoned and chopped)*
- 1 cup Tomatoes
- 0.25 cup Ginger *(ground)*
- 0.25 tbsp. Cayenne/Red Pepper or Chili Flakes/Powder
- 6 cups (1.4 liter) Brown Vinegar

Method:

- In a pan, boil the cored apples in vinegar till they become quite soft.
- Add all the other ingredients to the pan.
- Boil for around 30 – 45 minutes.
- Bottle the chutney when cold.

Wedding Cake

Ingredients:

- 3 cups Flour *(sifted)*
- 3 cups Butter
- 3 cups Sugar
- 4 cups Currants
- 2 cups Sultanas
- 1 cup Cherries
- 1.5 cups Almonds
- 1 cup Plums
- 1 cup Citron/Lemon Peel
- Pinch of salt
- 10 eggs
- 10 tbsp. Noyau/Almond extract
- 14 tbsp. Brandy
- Caramel *(as required)*

Method:

- In a big bowl, cream the butter and sugar together until the mixture become white.
- To this mixture, add in the eggs and the sifted flour alternatively while beating.

- Add the fruits, brandy and Noyau to the cake batter.

- To provide a lovely pale brown color to the final cake, add some caramel as needed.

- Pour the mixture into a tin, lined with several layers of buttered paper.

- Bake for the first 20 minutes at 350°F (176°C).

- Bake at 300°F (150°C) for the next 7 - 8 hrs.

- Garnish and serve the cake with a layer of Almond Paste *(recipe provided above)*.

Tips:

- To prevent the cake from burning, tie a thick layer of brown paper around the outside of the tin during baking.

- To make a three tiered cake, three times the quantities will be used of the above ingredients e.g. 30 tbsp. of Almond Icing will be required.

SHEPHERD'S PIE

Ingredients:

- 1 cup Meat of your choice *(cooked)*
- 1 cup Potatoes *(cooked)*
- 1 small Onion
- Stock/Gravy *(as required)*
- 1 tbsp. Butter/Shortening/Dripping
- Milk *(as required)*
- Salt and pepper *(to taste)*

Method:

- Mince the meat.
- Put the meat in a pie dish with some gravy or stock.
- Mash the potatoes and add the butter and milk.
- Cover the meat with the potatoes.
- Make pie marks round the edge of the pie. Brush over the top layer with milk.
- Bake in an oven at 350°F (176°C) until its brown all over and cooked through.

Tips:

- For the meat component, cooked and browned hamburger can also be used as a good alternative for those on a budget.

- The top layer of the pie can be made smooth with a knife or piped on with a bag.

BREAD PUDDING

Ingredients:

- 0.5 cup stale Bread
- 2 tbsp. Suet/Butter/Dripping/Shortening
- Raisins *(as required)*
- 1 tbsp. Sugar
- 10 tbsp. Milk
- 1 Egg
- Nutmeg *(as required)*

Method:

- Soak the bread in cold water. Squeeze it dry.
- Put a layer of bread into a greased pie-dish.
- Add a layer of suet or dripping, sugar and raisins to the dish over the bread.
- Repeat the above steps of adding a layer of bread and then a layer of suet, sugar and raisins until the dish is nearly full.
- Grate on a little nutmeg on the top layer.
- Beat the egg and mix it with the milk. Pour it on the top layer.
- Bake the pudding in the oven 300°F (150°C) for about 45 minutes (check after ½ hour).

Christmas Pudding

Ingredients:

- 2 cups Raisins
- 2 cups Currants
- 1 cup Sultanas
- 2 cups Suet/Butter/Dripping/Shortening
- 2 cups Bread Crumbs
- 1.5 cup Mixed Peel
- 1 small Nutmeg
- 0.25 tsp. Cinnamon *(ground)*
- 0.5 cup Almonds
- 1 cup Sugar
- 10 eggs
- 2 cups Milk
- 0.5 cup Brandy
- 0.5 cup Treacle/Golden Syrup
- Pinch of Salt

Method:

- Mix all the ingredients together and pour into buttered tin-basins.
- Cover with greased paper and tie-on cloths.

- Boil for 9 to 12 hours.

SCONES

Ingredients:

- 1 cup Flour
- 2 tbsp. Butter/Lard/Shortening/Vegetable Oil
- 0.5 tsp. Baking Soda
- 1 tsp. Cream of Tartar
- Pinch of Salt
- 1 tsp. Sugar
- 2 tbsp. Sultanas
- 0.5 cup Sour Milk/Buttermilk

Method:

- In a big bowl, mix the butter and the flour.
- Add the cream of tartar, salt, sugar and sultanas to the bowl.
- Dissolve the baking soda in the milk. Add it to the flour mixture.
- Mix the flour mixture well. Knead it to a soft dough.
- Half the dough and make two balls. Cut them across to form three-cornered scones.
- Bake on greased sheet at 356°F (180°C) for 10 – 15 minutes.
- When the scones are half baked, brush each over with milk for a glaze.

SHORTBREAD

Ingredients:

- 1 cup Flour
- 12 tbsp. Butter
- 4 tbsp. Sugar
- Pinch of Salt

Method:

- In a bowl, sift the flour and salt.
- Add the sugar to the bowl and mix in the butter.
- Knead it until smooth.
- Shape the dough into a ball. Pinch the edges with the thumb and first finger.
- Put it on a greased/buttered baking sheet with several layers of buttered paper under it.
- Tie a band of stiff buttered paper around the outside of the batter and prick the top.
- Bake in a slow oven 300°F (150°C) for about 45 minutes.

TRIFLE

Ingredients:

- 6 to 8 Sponge Cakes
- 2 Eggs
- 2 Egg Yolks
- 2 tbsp. Sugar
- Jam *(Apricot or any other of choice)*
- 1 cup Milk
- 1 cup Cream
- 0.5 cup Ratafias/Fruit Liqueur
- 0.5 cup Sherry
- 2 tbsp. Brandy
- 2 tbsp. Almonds
- 4 tbsp. Fresh/Preserved Fruits *(of your choice)*
- Vanilla *(as required)*

Method:

- Cut the sponge cakes and spread with jam.
- Put them together again and arrange them in a glass dish. Pour the ratafias.
- Pour the sherry and brandy and soak the cakes well.
- In another bowl, make custard with the two whole eggs and the 2 extra egg yolks. Stir the custard until it thickens.

- Sweeten and flavor the custard with vanilla. Allow it to cool.

- Just before serving, pour the custard over the cakes.

- Whip the cream and add the sugar.

- Decorate with preserved or fresh fruits and almonds.

Note: Recipe makes enough for 8 to 10 people.

Irish Stew

Ingredients:

- 2 cups Neck of Mutton
- 4 cups Potatoes *(sliced)*
- 2 cups Onions *(chopped)*
- Stock/Water *(as required)*
- Salt and pepper *(to taste)*

Method:

- Wipe the meat, chine it and cut it into chops.
- In a pot, add the potatoes and onions into layers to the meat.
- Add plenty of salt and pepper.
- Add a little stock or water.
- Simmer gently till the meat is cooked.

Note: Recipe makes enough for 5 to 6 people.

WELSH RAREBIT

Ingredients:

- 6 tbsp. Cheese *(grated)*
- 2 tbsp. Butter
- 0.5 tsp. Mustard
- 2 tbsp. Milk
- Salt and pepper *(to taste)*
- Buttered toast

Method:

- Add all the ingredients in a saucepan.
- Stir over heat until smooth.
- Pour over rounds of buttered toast and serve hot.

Apple Cider

Preparation Method:

- Gather fully ripe apples and store them in a loft for 2 weeks so that they become mellow.
- Crush the apples to a pulp and put them in a strong, coarse bag.
- Using a heavy weight, press out the juice into a large open tub. Keep the juice at a temperature of about 60 degrees.
- When the sediment has settled, rack the liquor off into a clean cask and stand in a cool place till the following spring.

Bottling Method:

- If the cider is not perfectly clear, clarify it and let stand for another 10 to 14 days.
- When clear, withdraw the bung and let it remain for 12 hrs.
- Fill the cider into bottles and leave them uncorked for a day.
- If the cider is required immediately, put a small piece of sugar in each bottle.
- Keep the bottles in a cool cellar.

Preserving Method:

- To keep the cider sweet, add 4 cups of pure refined linseed or olive oil.

Tips:

- After drawing all the cider, the oil can be saved and used for other purposes.

FISH AND CHIPS

Ingredients:

- Fish fillets
- 4 tbsp. Flour
- 1 tbsp. Oil/Butter
- 2 tbsp. tepid Water
- 1 Egg White
- Salt and pepper *(to taste)*
- Potatoes for Chips

Method (for Fish):

- Wash and dry the fish fillets.
- Add the flour, salt, and oil in a deep dish. Mix till smooth.
- Add tepid water and let the mixture stand for a while.
- Just before using, add the egg white using a beater.
- Dip in each fillet and coat it well.
- Fry the fillets in hot oil till they are done.
- Drain well and garnish with fried parsley.

Method (for Chips):

- Peel the potatoes and cut into thin slices.
- Dry the chips in a folded cloth and keep them covered until needed.

- Fry some of the chips in hot oil a few minutes. Add them few at a time.
- Drain the fried chips and put them in another pan of smoking hot oil to make them crisp.
- Drain them well.
- Sprinkle with salt and pepper and serve.

Tips:

- If only there is only one frying pan, let the oil get several degrees hotter to let the chips become crisp.

COOKING CONVERSION CHARTS

VOLUME CONVERSIONS

1/4 teaspoon (tsp) = 1.25 ml	1/2 tsp = 2.5 ml
1 tsp = 5 ml	1 tablespoon (tbsp) = 15 ml
1/4 cup = 60 ml	1/3 cup = 75ml
1/2 cup = 125ml	2/3 cup = 150 ml
3/4 cup = 175 ml	1 cup = 250 ml
1 1/8 cups = 275 ml	1 1/4 cup = 300 ml
1 1/2 cups = 350 ml	1 2/3 cups = 400 ml
1 3/4 cups = 450 ml	2 cups = 500 ml
2 1/2 cups = 600 ml	3 cups = 750 ml
3 2/3 cups = 900 ml	4 cups = 1 liter

OVEN/HEAT CONVERSIONS

Fahrenheit	Celsius	Oven Heat	Gas Mark
225°	110°	very cool	¼
250	120	very cool	½
275	140	cool	1
300	150	cool	2
325	160	moderate	3
350	180	moderate	4
375	190	moderately hot	5
400	200	moderately hot	6
425	220	hot	7
450	230	very hot	8
475	240	very hot	9

MISC. MEASUREMENTS

1 Wineglass	1/4 cup
1 Jigger	1.5 ounces
1 Gill	1/2 cup
1 Tea cup	3/4 cup (ish)
1 Coffee cup	1 cup (ish)
1 Tumbler	1 cup
1 Pint	2 cups
1 Quart	4 cups
1 Peck	2 gallons
1 Dash/Pinch	Take thumb and finger and pick up
1 penny weight	1/20 ounce
60 drops	1 teaspoon
1 drachma	1/8 ounce

COOKING SUBSTITUTIONS

1 cup sifted all purpose flour = 1 cup unsifted all purpose flour minus 2 tablespoons or = 1 1/4 cups sifted cake and pastry flour.
1 cup cake and pastry flour = 1 cup minus 2 tbsp all-purpose flour.
1 cup sifted self-rising flour = 1 cup sifted all-purpose flour plus 1 1/2 tsp baking powder and 1/2 tsp salt.
1 tbsp cornstarch (for thickening) = 2 tbsp flour or = 2 tsp quick cooking tapioca.
1 tsp baking powder = 1/4 tsp baking soda plus 3/4 tsp cream of tartar.
1 tsp double-acting baking powder = 1 1/2 tsp phosphate baking powder or = 2 tsp tartrate baking powder.

1 cup butter = 1 cup margarine (hard/brick type) or = 1 cup shortening.
1 cup liquid honey = 1 1/4 cups sugar plus 1/4 cup liquid.
1 cup corn syrup = 1 cup sugar plus 1/4 cup liquid.
1 cup granulated sugar = 1 cup brown sugar, firmly packed or = 1 1/3 cups brown sugar.
1 cup buttermilk or sour milk = 1 tbsp lemon juice or vinegar in a 1 cup measure plus add milk to make the 1 cup. Let stand 5 minutes.
1 cup buttermilk = 1 cup plain yogurt.
1 cup sour cream = 1 cup plain yogurt.
1 cup milk = 1/2 cup evaporated milk plus 1/2 cup water.
1 cup skim milk = 3 tbsp skim milk powder plus 1 cup water.
1 cup cream = 3/4 cup milk plus 1/4 cup butter.
1/2 cup oil = 1/2 cup melted butter or = 1/2 cup solid shortening, melted.
1 ounce chocolate (1 square) = 3 tbsp cocoa plus 1 tbsp butter or shortening.
1 package active dry yeast = 1 tbsp active dry yeast or = 1 cake of compressed yeast.
1 whole egg (approximately 1/4 cup) = 2 egg yolks plus 1 tbsp water. Omit the water for custards and similarly textured food.
1 cup meat stock (e.g. beef broth) = 1 cup consommé or canned meat

broth.
1 cup meat stock = 1 bouillon cube dissolved in 1 cup hot water or = 1 tsp instant bouillon.
4 cups chicken stock = 1 4 to 5 pound chicken, boiled for stock or = 4 cups canned broth or = 4 tsp instant chicken bouillon. Another cooking substitution would be 4 instant bouillon cubes plus 4 cups of water.
1 cup tomato juice = 1/2 cup tomato sauce plus 1/2 cup water.
1 cup tomato sauce = 1/2 cup tomato paste plus 1/2 cup water.
1 cup ketchup = 1 cup tomato sauce plus 1/2 cup sugar plus 2 tbsp vinegar.
1 clove garlic = 1/8 tsp garlic powder or 1/2 tsp garlic salt.
2 tbsp fresh chopped green or red pepper = 1 tbsp dried pepper flakes.
1 tsp dry mustard = 1 tbsp prepared mustard.
1 small onion = 1/4 cup chopped or = 1 tbsp dehydrated minced onion or = 1 tbsp onion salt.
1 tbsp fresh herbs (e.g. parsley or basil) = 1 tsp dried.
Juice of 1 lemon = 3 to 4 tbsp bottled lemon juice.
1/3 cup rum = 1 tbsp rum flavoring.

"No matter how big or small, acts of kindness are never wasted. With every gesture, with every step we can all make a difference in someone's life."

If you have the time to leave a positive review, it would be most gratefully appreciated.

Thank you kindly for your support...God Bless.

Made in the USA
Coppell, TX
05 December 2024